Humanity

Humanity

The Fallible Amphibian

KEN BAZYN

RESOURCE *Publications* • Eugene, Oregon

HUMANITY
The Fallible Amphibian

Copyright © 2019 Ken Bazyn. All rights reserved. Except for brief quotations in critical publications or reviews, no part of this book may be reproduced in any manner without prior written permission from the publisher. Write: Permissions, Wipf and Stock Publishers, 199 W. 8th Ave., Suite 3, Eugene, OR 97401.

Resource Publications
An Imprint of Wipf and Stock Publishers
199 W. 8th Ave., Suite 3
Eugene, OR 97401

www.wipfandstock.com

PAPERBACK ISBN: 978-1-5326-7026-8
HARDCOVER ISBN: 978-1-5326-7027-5
EBOOK ISBN: 978-1-5326-7028-2

Manufactured in the U.S.A. 01/10/19

Contents

Acknowledgments | ix
Introduction | xi

Always the Flaw | 2

Homo Sapiens | 5

On Human Nature | 8

Life Is … | 11

The Longer I Live | 14

The Fire Sermon | 16

The Selected Sayings of Confucius | 19

Too Bright Are Our Infirm Desires | 24

All Things Wind Down | 27

In the Words of Aurelius | 30

Entropy | 34

1985, or Life in the Suburbs | 37

Pleasantries | 40

The President's Dilemma | 42

For Chelsea | 44

On Persuading | 47

The Clapper | 49

Paralysis | 52

The Number of Man | 54

Powder Keg Assertions | 56

Why Call It a "Road"? | 58

Fortress Mentality | 61

A Crystal Chandelier | 64

Babel | 66

Semper Idem | 68

A Flatlander | 70

The Mechanical Thinking Marvel | 72

Evil's Impotence | 75

Postures | 78

Long-Awaited Rendezvous | 81

Blinding Revelation | 84

Half-Light | 87

Who Will Pass Judgment? | 90

To Be a Woman | 93

The Whimpering Victim | 95

THE WRONGED | 98

Civilized? | 99

"Jew-das" | 101

The Orchestra at Auschwitz | 104

East of Eden | 106

Trinity Site, New Mexico | 109

Death | 112

The Soul & the Body | 115

Prisoners of Time | 117

The Cosmic Fall | 120

Free Will | 124

Questions | 127

Solitude | 129

All I Have | 132

The Snow Falls Indifferently | 134

Unapproachable Light | 137

Listing of Photographs | 139
Works Cited | 143

Acknowledgments

I would like to thank those who have significantly contributed to this book, from my wife, Barbara, who offered numerous critical comments and worthwhile suggestions, to David Reynolds, who raised sharp stylistic questions and carefully proofread each line.

It's so exciting to see Wipf & Stock's growing list of high quality poetry. I appreciate Stephanie Hough for her typesetting expertise, Robert Meier for the care with which he developed my black-and-white 35mm film, and Rockbrook Camera in Omaha for taking these negatives and turning them into a splendid CD.

I also need to recognize one publication for first publishing a poem:
"Death" in *Cresset*

Introduction

The Riddle of Human Nature

"What a chimera then, is man!" exclaimed the seventeenth-century French polymath Blaise Pascal, who is credited, among other things, with devising the first calculating machine and founding the modern theory of probability. "What a novelty! What a monster, what a chaos, what a contradiction, what a prodigy! Judge of all things, imbecile worm of the earth: depositary of truth, a sink of uncertainty and error; the pride and refuse of the universe!"[1] Mankind, according to Alexander Pope in his famous "Essay on Man," is "the glory, jest, and riddle of the world!"[2]

How does one do justice to the heights and depths of human nature, its awesome achievements, its gross perversions? Christian tradition, in its wisdom, has acknowledged both extremes. Humankind is as moody as that romantic in Goethe's *Egmont*: "*Himmelhoch jauchzend,/Zum Tode betrübt*" (rejoicing to heaven, grieving to the point of death).[3] As Augustine so keenly recognized in the greatest autobiography from the ancient world, "*mihi quaestio factus sum*" (I have become a puzzle to myself).[4]

Even a rudimentary glance at history makes it clear that natural man is capable of advanced civilization; it is equally clear that man can wreak unimaginable havoc. Consider such legendary feats of engineering as the pyramids of Egypt, Iran's Persepolis, Rome's Pantheon, the Great Wall of

---

1. Pascal, *Pensées* and *Provincial Letters*, 143.
2. Pope, *Selected Poetry and Prose*, 139.
3. Goethe, *Selected Verse*, 47 (From Clare's song in the third act of *Egmont*). Cf. Goethe, *Egmont*, 45–46.
4. Augustine, *Confessions*, 154–55; Cf. Jaspers, *Plato and Augustine*, 71.

INTRODUCTION

China, Cambodia's Angkor Wat, Peru's Machu Picchu, and India's Taj Mahal.[5] Leaf through the extraordinarily varied listings of UNESCO World Heritage cultural sites scattered on every continent.[6]

Mapping the human genome was one of the greatest modern scientific undertakings, involving ten years of labor by more than two thousand scientists, who deciphered the 3.1 billion base pairs of DNA arrayed across twenty-four chromosomes.[7] Or what of Alexander Fleming's discovery of penicillin—ever since, medical researchers have been raising cultures of mold and synthesizing antibiotics to relieve untold suffering and pain. On the other hand, America's Manhattan Project employed one hundred and thirty thousand people during World War II and cost nearly $2 billion; it unleashed nuclear fission explosions over Hiroshima and Nagasaki, resulting in mega-mega deaths. In Germany, meanwhile, modern transportation, logistics, chemicals, and engineering led to the extermination of millions of "undesirables" like gypsies, homosexuals, and, primarily, Jews.

While one person may heroically rescue a sleeping child from a burning building, another will light the kindling beneath a suspected witch, based on the flimsiest of evidence. This lump of clay can be animated by the overweening ambition of a Genghis Khan, the saintly humility of a St. Francis, the sadistic cruelty of a Marquis de Sade, or the non-violent resistance of a Gandhi. The protagonists in world literature, too, range from never-at-a-loss Odysseus to tilter-at-windmills Don Quixote, from Faust's lust for forbidden knowledge to Underground Man's cynical loathing.

Should you want to observe these contradictions combined in a single person, consider that distinguished Renaissance goldsmith/sculptor, Benvenuto Cellini. Hypersensitive, he engaged in a lifelong series of brawls, in which he wounded, maimed, and even killed those he perceived to be opponents. His bragging knew no bounds; concerning his service as a gunner for Pope Clement VII during the sack of Rome, he claimed, "If I told in detail the great things I did in that cruel inferno, I would astonish the world."[8] Ever the hero of his autobiography, whether it be in art, romance, or war, the only rounded character he was capable of drawing was himself. Yet he showed deep loyalty to patrons (e.g., popes) and mentors (e.g., Michelangelo), as well as kindness to subordinates (e.g., his craftsmen). His

---

5. Cowan, *Guide to the World's Greatest Buildings*.
6. UNESCO, *World Heritage Sites*.
7. Collins, *Language of God*, 124.
8. Cellini, *Autobiography*, 76. See also introduction.

Introduction

masterworks, the gold and enamel saltcellar for King Francis I of France and the bronze statue of Perseus for the duke's palace in Florence, are still held in high esteem, while his careful descriptions of the lost-wax method of bronze casting are still much referred to. He had an extravagant writing style, enlivened by puns and allusions to Scripture. And, perhaps not surprisingly, in one vision given to him in prison, God appears—completely vindicating his zigzag character.[9]

I am fond of English essayist Thomas Browne's description of humanity as "that great and true *Amphibium*."[10] In the Book of Genesis, God formed Adam from the dust of the earth, then breathed into his nostrils till he became a living being (Gen. 2:7). Hence, we consist of both matter and spirit, capable of deep communion with God. In botanist Linnaeus' famous classification of all flora and fauna, he observed little anatomical difference between *Homo sapiens* and orangutans—except for the endowment of reason.[11] Pascal divided reason itself into *l'esprit de géométrie* and *l'esprit de finesse*; one being systematic and deductive, the other intuitive; one leading to science, the other to art.[12]

Closely related to this, of course, is language, and our ability to speak and write (Gen. 2:19; 3:2, 10). In recent years, linguist Noam Chomsky has strongly argued that infants are born with a device for processing rules of grammar—a capability unknown in other animals.[13] Significant, too, in Genesis, is humanity's internal moral compass (or conscience), by which we either obey or disobey God (Gen. 2:16-17). We have been created a little lower than the angels, says Psalm 8, crowned with honor and glory, and given dominion over the other beasts. Being a social creature, Adam required a companion, so God fashioned Eve, his wife, from one of his ribs (Gen. 2:18-25). Together, they assumed the mantle of joint-caretakers of the planet (Gen. 1:26).

During our long subsequent sojourn, immense changes have taken place. Humans have gone from being nomads, who wandered seasonally from place to place dependent on available food, to settled farmers who could domesticate animals, vegetables, grains, and fruit. To paraphrase the chorus in Sophocles's *Antigone*, there are many wonders on earth, but none

---

9. Brown, *Reader's Companion to World Literature*, 81-82.
10. Endicott, *Prose of Sir Thomas Browne*, 41-42.
11. Dunning, *Extremes: Reflections on Human Behavior*, 1.
12. Tournier, *Meaning of Persons*, 123. Cf. Pascal, *Pensées*, 210-12.
13. Blakemore, *Mechanics of the Mind*, 133-41. Cf. Chomsky, *Reflections on Language*.

is more wonderful than man. He can cross the wildest seas, plow furrows through the coarsest soils. Birds, he can snare, haul fish up with his nets, make pets of almost any wild creature.[14] If you post a sign saying "impossible," he simply considers it a challenge. For he has climbed twenty-nine thousand foot Mount Everest, descended to the bottom of the thirty-six thousand foot Marianas Trench, even orbited, and set foot on, the moon, two hundred and thirty-seven thousand miles away. He has been able to flourish in almost every conceivable ecological niche (hot/cold, wet/dry, windy/calm), within structures that create artificial climates.

So perhaps we should recognize adaptability (or plasticity) as our most impressive trait.[15] Dolphins are born swimming; giraffes learn to stand within hours; a baby zebra can run within forty-five minutes of birth; while a human baby emerges from the womb unable to fend for itself. Compared with the brains of other animals, ours is surprisingly malleable, unfinished. After the multitude of choices we had in early childhood, our options start to shrink, until a few become deeply ingrained.[16] Habits (programs burned into the structure of our brains) make multi-tasking easy, whether it be talking while driving or whistling while standing on tiptoe.[17] Indeed, Confucius's centuries-old maxim now seems prescient: "By nature, men are nearly alike; by practice, they get to be wide apart." He is, in effect, paying tribute to the pliability of human nature.[18]

One vital key is curiosity. French essayist Montaigne advised, "Put into his [a child's] head an honest curiosity to inquire into all things; whatever is unusual around him he will see: a building, a fountain, a man, the field of an ancient battle, the place where Caesar or Charlemagne passed."[19] Drop him into some new environment, he will land on his feet—eating local foods, picking up local customs, beginning to learn the local vocabulary—a survivor indeed!

Filmmaker Woody Allen's fictional character Zelig is as an apt metaphor for humanity's incredible range, which Montaigne describes as

---

14. Sophocles, *Three Theban Plays*, 76.
15. Gould, *Ever Since Darwin*, 257.
16. Eagleman, *The Brain*, 6–7.
17. Eagleman, *The Brain*, 89, 192.
18. Confucius, *Confucian Analects*, 318. Cf. Stevenson and Haberman, *Ten Theories of Human Nature*, 29.
19. Frame, *Montaigne's Essays*, 47.

"oscillation and inconsistency."[20] Zelig is called "a human chameleon. Like the lizard that is endowed by nature with a marvelous protective device that enables it to change color and blend in with its immediate surroundings, Zelig, too, protects himself by becoming whomever he is around." Leonard Zelig even undergoes dramatic physical and racial transformations—from Chinese to Caucasian, white gangster to black trumpeter.[21]

In real life, of course, we must deal with limitations, for we are all finite. "Time," allowed Thoreau, "is but the stream I go a-fishing in."[22] We cannot travel faster than the speed of light, Einstein insists,[23] so galaxy-hopping appears unlikely in our near future, unless quantum physics's idea of *entanglement* across great distances should somehow prove technologically feasible.[24] While we moderns speak of "eradicating" diseases, the truth is that new strains of virus are never far from breaking out of our chemical stays. And which of us will reach a hundred years old? Death comes to all. In his short story, *Ligeia*, Poe spoke of life as a play, "the tragedy, 'Man,'/And its hero the Conqueror Worm."[25]

The great Enlightenment philosopher Immanuel Kant argued that all that we can know is the world "as it appears to us," not "as it is in itself," since our perception and mental constructs filter objective reality.[26] Every judgment we make, observed fifteenth-century philosopher Nicholas of Cusa, is only based on comparisons with what we know and have seen.[27] Furthermore, our senses grasp but a narrow spectrum of available information. Visible light, for example, is a tiny fraction of the entire electromagnetic spectrum; radio waves, microwaves, X-rays, gamma rays, Wi-Fi, cell phone conversations, etc., flow through us continuously, yet apparently do not register. We just have no receptors to pick up their signals. Snakes, on the other hand, are equipped with heat sensors; birds can orient themselves to earth's magnetism; sharks recognize changes in the electrical field;

---

20. Frame, *Montaigne's Essays*, 147.
21. Allen, *Three Films of Woody Allen*, 33, 16, 12.
22. Thoreau, *Walden or, Life in the Woods*, 71.
23. Gardner, *Relativity Explosion*, 39. Cf. Einstein, *Relativity: The Special and General Theory*.
24. Clegg, *God Effect: Quantum Entanglement*.
25. Poe, *Complete Stories and Poems*, 102.
26. Stevenson and Haberman, *Ten Theories of Human Nature*, 114. Cf. Kant, *Groundwork*, 118–19.
27. Nicholas of Cusa, *Selected Spiritual Writings*, 88.

Introduction

crocodiles sense wave vibrations in water; elephants are able to hear at great distances; dogs know a richly-scented reality; and a few animals even see in ultraviolet. Each creature experiences only a slice of reality, but like us, probably assumes that is all there is.[28]

Our understanding is frail, flimsy; and more importantly, our wills are perverse. Genesis 3 points out how humanity has fallen—with far-reaching, cosmic implications. "God makes all things good; man meddles with them and they become evil," that eminent Romantic Rousseau noticed. Man "destroys and defaces all things; he loves all that is deformed and monstrous; he will have nothing as nature made it."[29] "We are not onely *passive*, but *active*, in our owne *ruine*," asserts seventeenth-century poet and clergyman John Donne. "We doe not onely stand under a *falling house*, but *pull* it downe upon us; and wee are not onely *executed* . . . but wee are *executioner* . . . and *executioners of our selves*."[30] Dostoyevsky's Underground Man goes one step farther, noting that "man likes to make roads and to create, that is a fact beyond dispute. But why has he such a passionate love for destruction and chaos also?"[31]

Reason alone just cannot fathom these evil inclinations. We play a dangerous game of hide-and-seek with ourselves.[32] "Nor will this overwhelming tendency to do wrong for the wrong's sake, admit of analysis, or resolution into ulterior elements," affirmed the narrator of Poe's short story, *The Imp of the Perverse*. "If there be no friendly arm to check us," we would quite likely plunge headlong into the abyss and be destroyed.[33] Freud, too, was continually struck by our conscious and unconscious aggression. A neighbor might actually help us, prove to be a wonderful companion, but he is also someone we could exploit. We can seize his possessions, humiliate, torture, and kill him: "*Homo homini lupus*,"[34] Freud summarizes, adapting a line from the Roman playwright Plautus: "man is a wolf to man."[35]

Dostoyevsky graphically illustrates just how irrational and destructive our actions can be in his greatest novel, *The Brothers Karamazov*. There

---

28. Eagleman, *The Brain*, 63–64, 185.
29. Rousseau, *Emile*, 5.
30. Coffin, *Poetry and Selected Prose of John Donne*, 457.
31. Dostoyevsky, *Three Short Novels*, 52–53.
32. Tournier, *Meaning of Persons*, 142.
33. Poe, *Complete Stories and Poems*, 272, 274.
34. Freud, *Civilization and Its Discontents*, 58.
35. Ehrlich, *Amo, Amas, Amat and More*, 144.

Introduction

Fyodor Pavlovich, that scoundrel of a father, recalls how "he had once been asked: 'Why do you hate that man so much?' And, in a fit of clownish shamelessness, he had replied: 'I'll tell you why. It's true he has done nothing to me, but I played him a dirty trick, and as soon as I had done it, I at once hated him for it.'"[36] Thus theologian Reinhold Niebuhr once remarked that "the doctrine of original sin is the only empirically verifiable doctrine of the Christian faith."[37]

That founder of utilitarianism, Jeremy Bentham, was at a loss to know why his proposals for promoting "the greatest happiness of the greatest number of people" met such stiff resistance, until it dawned on him: "A clue to the interior of the labyrinth has been found: it is the principle of self-preference. Man, from the very constitution of his nature, prefers his own happiness to that of all other sentient beings put together."[38] Niebuhr agrees, "No man will ever be so intelligent as to see the needs of others as vividly as he recognizes his own, or to be as quick in his aid to remote as to immediately revealed necessities."[39]

"It is a rather pathetic aspect of human social life," Niebuhr declares, that conflict, based on opposition, "is a seemingly unavoidable prerequisite of group solidarity."[40] Total objectivity is impossible. "There is, in all exchange of ideas," Niebuhr asserts, "a certain degree of unconscious suppression of facts or inability to see all the facts."[41] Thus did American founding father James Madison counsel the young democracy "that all men, having power, ought to be distrusted to a certain degree."[42]

For full-fledged self-exploration, we need to take into consideration Freud's defense mechanisms, Jung's repressed shadow, Adler's will to power, and so on. Such complexes help make sense of the paradoxes and apparent hypocrisy in human behavior. Yet even these depictions are arbitrary and subjective, contends Christian psychiatrist Paul Tournier, for behind any theory, lies experience. "If a certain person favors liberty, that is because at a decisive moment in his life, crushed under the weight of a rigorist

---

36. Dostoyevsky, *Brothers Karamazov*, 98. Cf. Tavris and Aronson, *Mistakes Were Made*, 35.
37. Niebuhr, *Man's Nature and His Communities*, 24.
38. Bowring, *Works of Jeremy Bentham*, 80.
39. Niebuhr, *Moral Man and Immoral Society*, 28.
40. Niebuhr, *Moral Man and Immoral Society*, 48.
41. Niebuhr, *Moral Man and Immoral Society*, 245.
42. Rutland, *Papers of James Madison*, 98.

upbringing, he has met a sincerely liberal person whose message has broken into his heart with the dazzling brilliance of new-found truth. If another favors discipline, that is because just when he was slipping, through lack of constraint, on the downward path of disorder, a salutary call to self-mastery broke in upon him with the same ring of truth."[43] But instead of empathizing with those who differ from ourselves, too often we build walls, espouse a "biblical" or "Christian" worldview based on a patchwork of proof-texts we personally have found compelling, yet knowing in our heart of hearts how arbitrary our collection really is.

Liberal and conservative mindsets alike are wired for self-justification. The psychologists Carol Tavris and Elliot Aronson, in their eye-opening *Mistakes Were Made (But Not By Me): Why We Justify Foolish Beliefs, Bad Decisions, and Hurtful Acts*, found that "most people, when directly confronted by evidence that they are wrong, do not change their point of view or plan of action but justify it even more tenaciously."[44] As Sartre observed, we choose our advisers according to the advice we expect to receive from them.[45] And when we do make mistakes, we simply calm the cognitive dissonance that jars our feelings of self-worth by creating fictions to absolve us of responsibility, so restoring a belief in our own goodness and righteousness. In other words, we live by continuous self-deception.

Memory aids and abets our alibis. While some of what we believe is based on what has actually happened, portions have been pieced together from stories told to us by others or from mere conjecture meant to fill the gaps in our knowledge.[46] For there is no way that events in the world can be directly transmitted to, or recorded by, our brains. "We now know," neurologist Oliver Sacks writes, "that memories are not fixed or frozen, like Proust's jars of preserves in a larder, but are transformed, disassembled, reassembled, and re-categorized with every act of recollection."[47] Our present colors our past. So a single event can be understood differently at various stages in our life.[48] Perhaps we did something wrong, but then in re-evaluating the event over time, we decide it actually was not our fault. "Memories are often pruned and shaped with an ego-enhancing bias,"

---

43. Tournier, *Person Reborn*, 105.
44. Tavris and Aronson, *Mistakes Were Made*, 2.
45. Sartre, *Existentialism and Humanism*, 37.
46. Eagleman, *The Brain*, 27, 29.
47. Sacks, *Hallucinations*, 154.
48. Eagleman, *The Brain*, 25.

INTRODUCTION

Tavris and Aronson observe, "that blurs the edges of past events, softens culpability, and distorts what really happened."[49] Whenever we make a decision, our mind has a complete set of psychological tools to help bolster its reasoning. Should contradictory evidence be introduced, we either criticize or dismiss it.[50]

How much more fitting it would be, if our finiteness led to humility. Our life is but a vapor, or smoke, which appears briefly, then evaporates, says the Book of James (4:14).[51] "Homer calls a man 'a leaf,' the smallest, the weakest piece of a short-lived unsteady plant," notes seventeenth-century Anglican bishop Jeremy Taylor. "Pindar calls him 'the dream of a shadow.'"[52] Roman emperor and Stoic philosopher Marcus Aurelius viewed life as a mere pinpoint in infinite time, a knife-edge between two eternities. Our activities are "smoke and nothingness"; our prizes are "a bird flying past, vanished before we can grasp it"; the clash of armies like "the quarrel of puppies over a bone." Indeed, he compares his own triumph over the Sarmatians to a spider capturing a fly.[53]

To overcome self-deception and to make the most of our brief lives, let us pay attention to honestly-recorded stories of faithful figures in the past. Saints, G.K. Chesterton thought, are antidotes which restore the world to sanity by exaggerating what it neglects. He felt that each generation is converted by the saint who most contradicts it.[54] We are formed by what we admire; saints, like figures in stained-glass windows, are illuminated by a source outside themselves. Some have proven to be noteworthy spiritual guides, while others have lighted a torch for social activism. Some have risen to prominence, and others have labored in obscurity. While some have re-awakened long-dormant traditions, others have opened up virgin trails. Some received recognition and honor during their lifetimes; others were scorned, persecuted, and even slain.[55] Among them were apologists, theologians, missionaries, musicians, statesmen, artists, pastors, scientists,

---

49. Tavris and Aronson, *Mistakes Were Made*, 7–8.

50. Tavris and Aronson, *Mistakes Were Made*, 27, 21–22.

51. Davids, *Epistle of James*, 172.

52. Taylor, *Rule and Exercises*, 2. Cf. Homer, *Iliad*, 76–77. Lattimore, *Odes of Pindar*, 80.

53. Dodds, *Pagan and Christian*, 8. Cf. Aurelius, *Meditations*, 6:36; 10:31; 6:15; 5:33; 10:10.

54. Chesterton, *Saint Thomas Aquinas*, 23–24.

55. Ellsberg, *All Saints*, 475.

poets, reformers, scholars, and mystics.[56] Chesterton himself became best known for his Father Brown character, a priest/sleuth who was modeled after Chesterton's friend Father O'Connor. Due to years of hearing confessions, and a seasoned understanding of human nature, the fictional priest could sniff out the trail of a criminal with more acumen than any constable.[57]

The religious person, Niebuhr decided, "feeling himself under the scrutiny of an omniscient eye, and setting his puny will into juxtaposition with a holy and omnipotent will . . . is filled with a sense of shame for the impertinence of his self-centered life."[58] Religion enables us to face up to life's great quandaries: one's inevitable death, wrongdoings and failures, and the true meaning of existence.[59] Yet even here, Montaigne warned, charlatans abound. "I know of no quality so easy to counterfeit as piety, if conduct and life are not made to conform with it. Its essence is abstruse and occult; its semblance, easy and showy."[60]

According to Confucius, everyone is potentially a sage who is capable of acting with extreme benevolence (*ren*). We all have a capacity for cultivating virtue, bringing ourselves in harmony with the Decree of Heaven.[61] As gradually maturing Christians, we are purged of our shortcomings by daily taking up our cross (Matt. 16:24), so becoming "partakers of the divine nature" (2 Pet. 1:4 RSV). The human propensity to do evil, even "radical" evil, can be overcome, according to Kant's reckoning, through freedom of the will.[62] In John Steinbeck's re-enactment of the sorrowful tale of Cain and Abel in *East of Eden*, he contemplates God's warning to Cain: "sin is crouching at the door; its desire is for you, but you must master it" (Gen. 4:7 RSV). Lee, Adam's faithful Chinese servant, finds hope in the Hebrew phrase *timshel* (you may). The word carries with it, if not the promise, at the least the possibility of victory. "Thou *mayest* triumph over sin."

---

56. Editors of "Christian History" Magazine, *131 Christians Everyone Should Know*.

57. Chesterton, *Autobiography*, 321–24. Cf. Chesterton, *Penguin Complete Father Brown*.

58. Niebuhr, *Moral Man and Immoral Society*, 51.

59. Stevenson and Haberman, *Ten Theories of Human Nature*, 231.

60. Frame, *Montaigne's Essays*, 339.

61. Stevenson and Haberman, *Ten Theories of Human Nature*, 28.

62. Kant, *Religion*, 32. Cf. Stevenson and Haberman, *Ten Theories of Human Nature*, 123–24.

INTRODUCTION

"Surely most men are destroyed," Adam's neighbor asserted, "but there are others who like pillars of fire guide frightened men through the darkness. '*Thou mayest, Thou mayest!*' What glory!"[63] Indeed, if we do not make just such an effort, entirely dependent on God's grace, we will end up like those earth colonists in Ray Bradbury's *Martian Chronicles*, who go on bearing the same contagion to any future location, even after their own home planet has been annihilated.[64]

---

63. Steinbeck, *Novels 1942–1952*, 629–30, 635–6. "Timshel" (you may) is actually "timshol-bo" (you shall), a future tense command, in the Hebrew Bible. Cf. Babbage, *Mark of Cain*, 9–15.

64. Bradbury, *Martian Chronicles*, 177–81.

Always the Flaw

Always the flaw—right in the heart of the diamond,
Always the scratch near the center of the lens,
Always the excuses when you haven't the time,
Always the dark meat when you wanted the light,
Always the tears when you wished to be jolly,
Always the demands which postpone your nap,
Always the dreams that flutter away,
Always the rules which do not apply,
Always the moola—but it never lasts,
Always the whores if love you despise,
Always the bread that stales on your palate,
Always the wine—and it's never wasted,
Always the friends that sour in a season,
Always the faithful that pull down your masks,
Always the projectiles that veer from their courses,
Always the poor (and they need your compassion),
Always the prejudice in little green eyes,
Always the side wind that alters your perception,
Always the politicians who lie through their teeth,
Always the children who learn only by mistake,
Always the papers that arrive after the deadline,
Always the taboos surrounding the truth,
Always the God who splits you in half,

Always Jesus crucified, but what of his resuscitation?

Always the questions, yet who has the answers?

There are three Christs in Ypsilanti and none offer salvation.

Homo Sapiens

Fizzled out like mercury
or half-life of a thousand days,
man crawls, struts and then
hobbles to his grave,
a kiss, a hug, a sad adieu,
now exits, now burns a truer flame,
here we worried and sang,
thought of others more than took initiative,
speculated like a basket full of sophists,
earned our diplomas in mortality,
peopled the solar system with
transmitting toys, domesticated the
sweet potato and camel, invented
radio telescopes but little green
men never came, prolonged our
execution one more hour than we ought,
camouflaged the yolk in a cabalistic sac.

Born to wither, study but to forget,
a tale our parents concocted
from a moment's pleasure, sown in
grief and harvested in gloom,
an ephemeral vapor, a Ponce de León wish,

a comic interlude, a chance roll
of the die, up like mushrooms
did we spring, then the clouds formed,
insubstantial ghosts who dematerialized
whene'er the cock did crow,
a blot in an otherwise obedient universe
that can swiftly be erased,
a maelstrom that should be capped
before the world is harmed,
a flickering candle
that but shadowboxes with the wall,
a firecracker that was left out in the rain.

On Human Nature

As restless as the waves that strike Point Pleasant's rim
or Fundy's tide,
as forlorn as the whippoorwill,
as bereft of wisdom as the counselors of Job,
as exemplary as the mold that keeps the factory worker in stitching,
as cynical as Hobbes,
as devil-may-care as laughing Democritus,
as shallow as the cosmetic eye or tooth,
as petty as the troika when Caesar reigns,
as happy as the evergreen when winter assassinates the grass,
as polite as the spinning top when it finishes its dance,
as inebriate as the tumbler after a corkscrew prologue,
as topsy-turvy as the interim between now and the apocalypse,
as promiscuous as King Soma with 27 stars to wive,
as virtuous as the fire in Savonarola's Florence,
as awkward as the pistil after the petals go,
as cold-blooded as the salamander in Truman Capote's "novel,"[1]
as precise as the graduated beaker whose bottom rotted out,
as circumlocutious as the five-year-old's route to the cookie jar,
as fleeting as the rainbow when the colors drip away,
as unlettered as the Arunta tribesmen before the missionaries came,
as stiff-necked as the giraffe,

1. Capote, *In Cold Blood*.

as reprehensible as the noodle,

as decorative as the shook foil frappe,

as headstrong as Pizarro,

as Southern as corn pone,

as dubious as a $3 bill,

as petered out as a balloon.

Life Is . . .

Life is disillusionment
    criss-crossed with unfathomed grief,
a tankard of woe, forty lashes,
    a guillotine of Roman busts.

It is the cracked surface wherein
    we behold God's contorted face,
a Navajo sand painting
    that induces all to groan,
the kingdom of perpetual night.

Life is a flourish of the brush,
    a fading, pretty fresco
daubed in pastel decadence,
    scratched, unretouched,
a crazy palette heaved against the sky.

It is a gossamer engineering contraption
    honeyed with all the choicest lures,
like spiders bouncing on a trampoline,
    we pounce and sting,
then off to bed with our stomachs full.

Life is some sweet, short carnival,
    men dress like women, girls
undress before whomever they choose,
    priests bless felons, wicked sorcerers
are arrayed around the Holy Truth.

We squat, parrot, rest a bit,
    plot, get soused, evade our taxes,
some end up in Sing Sing or possibly Congress,
    like characters from an Oriental fairy tale
we o'ertake the throne, then are lulled into oblivion.

The Longer I Live

The longer I live
the more I'm convinced:
    man is a stray animal
    in a wounded universe.

In the ocean of his delusions,
man wanders all adrift,
hits a reef, founders,
his anchor shorn, his azimuth conjecture,
man navigates by dreams.

Sequestered in his eremitic cell,
man utters matins and lauds
to his amicus curiae;
convicted by internal evidence,
the defendant stands mute.

At nine o'clock man punches in,
reads his paper, smooths his desk,
chats with colleagues, sips his cup,
bombasts all who disagree,
distorts his statement, collects his check.

Man hems in his behavior with perfunctory rules,

can't try this, mustn't enjoy that,

his courage? o'ershadowed by his fears;

he ventures out to the gates of Hercules,

does a quick calculation, then retreats to his desk.

The Fire Sermon

The eye is on fire
as is the nose,
the mouth and reddened tongue,
the world is burning, burning,
the heavens, too,
the planets and flaming stars.

All that we see
is consumed, or being consumed,
all that we hear
is livid conflagration,
all that we smell
is strong as sulfur.

Our thoughts crackle,
our desires flicker like low-threshold kindling,
every crutch we lean on
becomes an ignited match,
the mountains are rimmed with lightning,
the prairies smoke like a citrus lantern.

I myself am all aglow,
lapping up dried sticks and twigs,

a kerosene-soaked candle
with a self-renewing wick:
how can my vigor be dampened,
my spark blown coolly out?

The Selected Sayings of Confucius[2]

Can anyone do good with all his might
for as long as an entire day?
I doubt it.
Rotting wood can't be carved,
nor can dried dung be troweled,
why should I reprove Tsai Yu[3] any further?

Everywhere I look nothing is pretending to be something,
what's empty pretending to be full,
—the best one can hope for
is to find a man of fixed principles.
In vain have I sought
someone who perceives his own faults,
then zealously corrects them,
or who's in full control of his sexual appetites.
Appoint those who are honest, place them above the crooked,
so is perverseness mitigated.

Do not do to others
what you wouldn't want them to do to you.
Conduct yourselves away from home,

    2. Inspired by Confucius, *The Analects*, in translations by Arthur Waley, James Legge, D.C. Lau, etc.
    3. A disciple in whom Confucius was disappointed.

as though in the presence of an honored guest.
Deal with all you meet
as though you were officiating at some major festival.

Listen much,
remain silent when in doubt,
be cautious with your lips and tongue.
To be poor and never murmur
is more difficult than to be rich and not overbearing.
A man who is not genuine—
what does he have to do with music?
Heaven intends for each of us
to be a gong or a clanging bell.

As Tseng Tzu asserts,
"When a bird dies, its notes are plaintive,
when a man dies, his final words are memorable."
At fifteen I set my heart on learning,
at thirty I placed my feet on firmer ground,
at forty I no longer wavered before metaphysical perplexities,
at fifty I knew the laws of Heaven,
at sixty I graciously submitted to their decrees,
at seventy I could follow the prompting of my own heart
without overstepping proper bounds.

Do not boast of a future action,
lest it prove beyond your powers.
It's true that Tzu Lu has entered the main hall,
but he has not penetrated the inner sanctum.

Tzu Kung declares, "I detest those who consider shrewdness wisdom,
those who perceive insolence as courage,
those who count gossiping as forthrightness."

If the water is deep,
find stones to step across;
if it is shallow,
lift up your robe.[4]
Upon recognizing the good, seize it,
lest it somehow elude you;
or if you notice a likely evil,
dip your finger in quickly
as though into a simmering kettle.

Anyone who purifies himself,
I will accept as a disciple,
although I can't be held accountable for his previous mistakes.
Only those who are enthusiastic to study, do I instruct,
nor have I turned away any because they were poor.
That one over there is no genuine follower of mine,
little children, bang the drum loudly
and assail him, I give you permission.[5]

The true *chun-tzu* is one to whom
I would entrust either a young orphan
or the sovereignty of a state,
even in a time of great crisis.

---

4. Waley, *The Book of Songs*, 54.
5. Said tongue-in-cheek.

His courage, wisdom, and goodness will soon become evident.

Such a one is like a consecrated vessel of jade;

he will never sour

if his talents aren't honored or appreciated—

like a cypress in winter,

when the year draws near its close,

he will be the last to lose his color.

Too Bright Are Our Infirm Desires

Beauty is forever sleeping in the fairy tales,
when it wakes, will it be as ugly as the Hydra?
Virtue, too, is cloistered, detached from this seething world,
when it enters into pain, shall it be piqued by internecine controversy?
on the mountaintop Faith is indefatigable,
yet in the valley, might it rust and lose its cutting edge?
blustery Courage has medals, trophy cases of the mind,
still, in the heat of battle, could it turn tail and run?

Sometimes flattering images must be delicately retouched
with harsh, somber, more realistic tones;
saints' miracles may be questioned, not a few haloes dropped;
exemplary kings can slip off their triumphal arches
when scholars rummage through an aide-de-camp's reminiscences;
even a poet's resonating voice may be devastated
by several false, loosely-plucked strings of the heart.

Not that superheroes can't exist,
but typically they appear with hyper-egos and truth-telling quirks;
not that trombones won't have a high, metallic ring,
but often they are diluted by dissonant woodwinds and percussions;
not that reefs and lagoons don't contain oysters and pearls,
yet how often one dives down and bobs up with gravel;

not that freedom, justice, and truth won't prevail,
but petty irritations and self-aggrandizing airs frequently interfere.

Between what is and what we long for
lie rubies and phantoms,
obviously we're attracted to the shapeliest and most succulent,
too bright are our infirm desires.

All Things Wind Down

All things wind down,
the pendulum takes its last tick,
rivers grow sluggish, form meanders and oxbows,
the sun will flare up in a fusion explosion,
collapse into starry debris,
I, too, am weary of incessant psychic tremors
pushing me to the precipice,
this vain striving for satisfaction must stop,
diabolical principles are at work.

Youth is crowned with gray follicles,
coursing fluids fill up with sediment,
trees lose their bark prematurely,
turn hollow, are burned up in a column of smoke,
churning headland breakers
grow weary, less agitated,
noisy gulls sleep quiet as death,
enfeebled atoms become too weak to bond
when inertia and gravity reach absolute parity,
butterflies re-enter staid old cocoons.

Solar-powered motors sputter, cough, and wheeze,
involuntary reflexes lose their elasticity,
food is swirled round and round by the tongue's bland blender,

light pulses intermittent, diffuse,

words crack under the larynx's strain,

the last decimal of pi eludes Alexandrian mathematicians,

spring, too, loses its oomph,

what once aroused passion, now excites envy,

there's nothing new under this quadrant of the sun,

as "I" incrementally ceases to be biological "me."

In the Words of Aurelius[6]

Earthly elements sink,

the watery converge and flow together,

fire rises,

airy substances appear as wisps of vapor,

gold and silver corrode,

the soul carries within the spores of its own dissolution.

So then live your life on a high mountain

indifferent to pleasure and pain,

fully aware that whatever happens

has been ordained for the good of the whole,

and is not contrary to the nature of man.

Since existence resembles a wrestling match more than a dance,

be ready for the sudden and unexpected.

Ask yourself:

what is this person's significance or that thing's essence?

what place does it occupy?

how long will it endure?

of which materials is it composed?

for whose advantage has it been established?

---

6. Inspired by Aurelius, *The Meditations*, in translations by G.M.A. Grube, George Long, Maxwell Staniforth, etc.

A bitter cucumber? Throw it out!
Briars on your path? Step around.
Don't inquire too deeply why such objects exist,
instead, dig within—for there's the ever-flowing fountain.
Your mind is a self-sufficient sphere.

Perform tasks for others,
but like an old man who is retrieving
a lost toy for his foster child,
recognizing the deed's near insignificance.

Do people offend?
They will go on in their propensities,
though you split yourself apart from anger.
Perhaps some portion of your behavior irritates them.
Think rather of what you admire in others;
never stoop to become like an enemy.
Let that wrong done to you soon be forgotten.

Should some idea enchant, overpower you,
lay bare the exalted language
which has made it proud,
then like a promontory—stand firm
amid the tumultuous waters.

Surely time is but a point—
and how small the nook where you live—
being is in flux, perception dull,

the body subject to infirmity and decay,
the soul a whirling eddy,
death either a scattering of atoms,
extinction, or a change of residence.
So, as if you've already died,
live the rest of your life as a bonus.

Everything that happens will recur—
whether at the courts of Antoninus, Philip, or Alexander—
today's flatterers are the same as those who have gone before,
though they evince a different set of features.
How many a Chrysippus, a Socrates, an Epictetus
has already been swallowed up by the ages?

Finally, recall the words of Heraclitus:
"the death of earth becomes water,
that of water, air,
that of air, fire,
and so on—for all eternity."
There was a yawning infinity before you were born,
another remains after you leave,
you embarked, set sail, reached harbor,
now disembark.
Was there ever anything that prevented you
from being either good or simple?

Entropy

Created more out of helium than lead,
our lives shoot up to the ceiling,
hesitate,
then in one fell swoop descend into the grave.

Entropy advances in columns of deterioration,
first the eyes go,
then the epidermis fails,
hairs drop out,
molars must wear a golden crown.

Joints creak, fatty tissue forms
'neath the midriff,
bones fracture,
knees totter,
memory traces are silted over,
blood vessels cart more waste than nutrients.

Metabolism comes to a crawl,
doctors set artificial limbs,
glands and enzymes
boost erroneous signals,
alarm sensors doze.

Every movement's catatonic
or monotonously repeated,
remembrance of the ritual,
oblivious of the source.

Circuits overheat,
sockets rust, spark plugs
show insufficient fire,
bolts loosen, the chassis wobbles,
batteries go kaput.

Our torn, leaking transmission
requires an outright overhaul.

1985, or Life in the Suburbs

A conventional life
in a conventional modular house,
second-hand ideas garnered
from shopping mall newspaper stands,
the latest fad in tamper-proof pillboxes,
have you read the excerpts from this month's bestseller?
seen the budget director's exposé in the *Atlantic*?
been to that hometown major upset football game?

This year children are enamored of computers, Trivial Pursuit,
next year they'll manufacture a new Cabbage Patch doll,
Lebanese terrorists are mocking our resplendent flag,
in the media there's a marked increase in airplane disasters,
Hollywood is riding the sci-fi craze,
Swedish cars are bourgeois in vogue:
no one buys Detroit—except maybe Chrysler,
are you in favor of abortion on demand?
Let's take a poll.

Eccentrics—that's what's un-American—
Christians quote from the same Bible society translation,
Jews have taken up street-corner evangelism,
in the melting pot all's Midwestern and bland,

dialects are dying out, regional distinctions,
ethnicity's a leftover from some bygone immigrant era,
Republicans, Democrats, neo-conservatives, ultra-liberals
all drink the same California Madeira, smoke a nicotine-laden Camel,
are afraid to appear
more learned, gifted, distinguished
than any other neighboring dolt.

Wow! A new situation comedy is climbing up Nielsen's,
50s-style rock music appeals to baby boomers,
Disney's studio has just released a second animated flop,
which do you prefer: the old Pepsi or the new Coke?
so life continues on in this serio-comic Tati greenbelt,
where clones keep cloning interchangeable clones in Eli Whitney factories.

Pleasantries

Pleasant thoughts pleasantly expressed,
surrounded by people so good of heart;
if they sin it's quite unintentional,
talking of pedigree dogs,
who's wearing what to the charity ball,
some new minister has just moved into town,
what warm weather we've been having,
Detroit's the team to watch this year.

Pleasantries are expressed, but who
screams from the bottom of his soul?
they go on with their banter—ignoring incest,
homophobia, sham politicians, bribed gendarmes,
wife-battering, the crisis in modern education, rampant incarceration—
they look the other way at snide remarks,
how contemptible to raise one's voice,
it's vulgar to express a contrary opinion.

They tell occasional off-color jokes,
assume everyone shares their middlebrow prejudices,
God damn the reformer,
nature can cure its own impurities,
if the poor only put their kids in private schools,

psychotics can convalesce with a garden and hoe,
a little discipline never hurt any delinquent,
how can anyone take nuclear proliferation seriously?

Disaster can happen—but never here.
You'd think this was a century of costume drama,
Jane Austen social mores, pastoral idyllic poetry,
instead of one of total annihilation.

The President's Dilemma

A moderate earthquake registers 5.9 on the Richter scale,
Mount Hood erupting, five-hundred people dead,
Arizona having the third-hottest summer on record,
and the President can't decide whether to use
his two-iron or driver on the 194-yard par three.

For Chelsea

Past mistakes keep winging their way back
like Monarchs to podded milkweed,
rash, misleading jibes,
friends equivocatingly betrayed,
misty goals I feared to tread,
overenthusiasm for simplistic solutions,
an unwillingness to yield when shown a correctable mistake,
I've wept much, expected other's pity for superficial wounds,
early on, got friendship mixed up with love,
never paid in full the outstanding debts
due the gentle, kindly folk where I grew up,
who steadied an awkward, hometown lad.

Yet there rooted an agreeable, self-effacing character
in a non-combative, rural Midwestern environment,
who was honed by reading and eager for self-discovery,
though willing to honor any with craftsman/technical talents,
sure that perseverance will overcome
all but the most debilitating handicaps,
seeing God as central to the universe's unfathomable core,
but to behave as if he gave no tangible rewards,
continuing my life, as faithful, in an uneventful corner,
as though it were played before a royal stage.

Hmm—I've started this poem
wallowing in self-contrition,
ended up in a paean to visages from the past,
Samuel Johnson grew convinced
that people were kinder than he imagined,
I, too, am mystified, stunned
by those who do me special favors,
for the law I can understand
and give it my wholehearted assent,
but grace always comes unexpectedly,
like a whoosh of wonder that ravishes.

On Persuading

Couldn't the world move closer

to what I believe?

undergo a traumatic conversion,

or douse my robust euphoria

with cold, wet facts?

Friends can't be persuaded;

relatives wade into unfamiliar pools,

step out intact again

—might geography determine all?

Who holds

the telltale angle?

I've studied columns

from the keenest commentators,

can cite row after row of fetching statistics,

slice through the outright posturing,

put the whole in a precise chronological sequence;

values don't change,

just their inflection.

I've marshaled convincing arguments
in a setting of Ciceronian bronze;
loyalty, however, transcends pure, golden reason,
is alloyed with unstable manganese, copper, and tin.

The Clapper

Shall we cut out the bell's
    sullen tongue—
pealing out unfeelingly
both laughter and despair?
    chiming to the sluggard:
hurry up, you'll be late.
    Festivities commence
regardless of titles, marquis,
coronations, weddings, stately processions,
calls to war, fire! anarchists in the street,
    those rites of passage
the church considers sacramentally significant.

The stupendous, vibrating chords
resemble medulla throbs of metallic pain
    or an alarm system for social insects
        —wasps, termites, honey bees.
Pedestrians stop to inquire:
    what banner headline
is our bronze tabloid announcing today?

Gossips whisper half-truths,
    municipal officials smile and nod

like omniscient clay idols,
children caught up in life-and-death games
    appear indifferent,
more deaf than the aged with canes,
    strangers wonder:
has some new inquisition broken out?

Yet that gong hammer
keeps pelting the sky
—brazen, disruptive, demandingly loud—
    in villages far from the main thoroughfares,
    where merchants trade second hand,
the mere hint of excitement
is clapper enough
    for several rude awakenings a week.

Paralysis

No paralysis is as fatal
as habitual indecision.

The Number of Man

This is the number of man:

.000 . . . 1—infinitesimal.

Powder Keg Assertions

Powder keg assertions—
apply a tincture of anger,
then watch her blow.

Why Call It a "Road"?

        Why call it a "road"?
                when it veers first this direction,
        then looping, slants back
      like a haphazard, crazy, drunken digression,
    while traversing point A to point B,
  it follows reverse-image schematics,
takes up allelic form,
meanders like some decrepit river.

  Why should there be a correlation
      between pinpoint geographical coordinates
        and release of the inner light?
          I call it the Little Gidding ruse,
            a mass hallucination in spatial grid—
              nebulous as a Seurat pointillist mosaic,
                indeterminate as Riemann's positive curvature.

        Observable—yes—quantifiable—perhaps—
      traceable even by stencil,
    still the atoms co-mingle promiscuously
  like a parody whorled up within a satire
or a limerick encapsulated within an uproarious witticism,
you might believe all to be weighty, of consequence,

plan for some ennobling encounter,
> but more likely you're moving from what's exterior, tangible,
>> to an internal, unbathyscaphed abyss.

Fortress Mentality

Harsh, implacable walls
where smiles recede
into stubborn, unblinking shadows—
inviolate, impervious as marble,
sheer as the crags and precipices around Beijing.
Why, what are you blocking out, screening, preventing;
what whimpering, imprisoned form
lies behind your unspoken anger?
Reply in a language I can comprehend
and vigorously dispute.

How sleepless your hair-trigger lookouts,
how shuttered those immovable doors,
your barbed wire tears flesh into strips like bacon,
your granite determination cloaks, partitions,
defeats all attempts at free civilized interchange.
You stand sober, vigilant,
alert as a Kurdistan rifleman,
defending monopoly trade routes or royal succession;
I long to breach your stiff-necked facade.

But, once inside, my superiors
would begin to repair, refortify,

till a new generation of grenadiers march past.

Walls sap my strength, my marrow,

with their false Maginot faces.

So, Joshua blow your terrifying trumpet,

Jericho is ripe as Khartoum.

Except the Lord take his turn on the tower,

the walls may as well be tissue or brittle, defective glass.

A Crystal Chandelier

A crystal chandelier
    dangles in the house
of merriment and greed,
    so piteous white and clear
like a callow Vanderbilt.

Underneath its mirrored gaze
    socialites slow step
and wed beyond their reach,
    tall, lascivious beaus
gather squishy, too-sweet fruit.

The unstained marble staircases,
    the immaculate, scissored grounds,
a trellised veranda with gargoyle cornices,
    there's a magnificent escutcheoned window
overlooking a picture-postcard bay.

Rasputnik! Park Avenue clientele!
    ornate, obese larvae,
so resplendent, so conscious of form,
    (even their jests are mimeographed for the occasion)
like suave, elegant shells.

Babel

Languages awry,
Bruegel, Peter the Elder,
fricatives, dentals, labials,
at the pyramids of Ur
men mouth congestion, confusion,
it were easier to escape the Minotaur
than to climb down with Nimrod,
if one could intuit Esperanto or Basic English,
invent a universal phoneme tongue,
we'd disgorge structuralists at breakfast,
excrete translators with snacks.

But as it is there are cutthroats and muggings,
violent monologues from the base to the tower,
we're pelted with "hi!" "how are ya?"
and it can't be unscrambled,
so all read in their own sinister motives,
French curves, daredevil loops, roller
coaster ups and downs, we puff and move our lips,
but all communication is at checkmate.

Semper Idem

Kikes, spics, and nigger-lovers,

Neolithic epithets, prejudice of uncreative minds,

lips that suck in pauper souls

and spew them out in cartoon capsules,

visages shut up by collective bigotry,

whirligig Chomsky larynx boxes,

the idiom of Shakespeare in the mouth of knaves,

decimating virtue with a rasping tongue,

tossing relatives into Tartarus,

consigning our foes to the ninth ring,

masquerading as libertarians—vilifying the human race,

projecting self-hate via an uvular trill,

stabbing each other in the back with pocket knives,

why, it's the very sport of pacifists, the amusement of professors,

plate glass sinners avenging imaginary slights,

sacrilegious offense! abomination to the temple ghost!

in a Hardyesque universe we need a whiff of grace.

A Flatlander

I have no room for new thought,
can't quite adjust to paradigm shifts
or any epochal dispensations,
revolutions leave me a fleeing refugee,
like a staid barnacle I yearn for encrustation,
seeing gravity as my truest friend.

Should someone cross my i's or dot my t's
I'm nearly a basket case for the asylum,
a quarter-turn and I'll lose my bearings,
having no perpendicular grid or reliable astrolabe,
I might as well be left blindfolded on the open prairie,
since my compass has its own curious flaws.

I hug the variegated grasses
as pyrite clinging to lodestone,
trampoline bouncings make me queasy,
I'm content to be a Flatlander all my days
with neither time warps nor hyperspace to consider,
fading featureless into a sinkhole of forgetfulness.

The Mechanical Thinking Marvel

The mechanical thinking marvel—
neurons snapping, electrons spinning,
serendipitous cybernetic patterns,
magnetic ferrite rings,
laser-illuminated photogravure—
savoring a coup de grâce at chess.

Artificial constructs, thermoplastic connectors,
is there some ghost in the machine?
facial muscles reminiscent of Darwin's animal expressions,
the only scratchy robotic sound
is the perpetual motion gears.

Questions must be plunked down the throat
for Edison filaments to blink,
paper spewed out in scrambled computerese;
for affinity between species to take place
codes must be deciphered, idiomatic expressions broken down,
logical equivalents proffered for any humor.

Are circadian biorhythms programmable?
if one half never sleeps, is the other in the trauma of dream,
do even noteworthy anthropologists come with cultural blinders?

And how can one define intelligence

peacock-preening before a selfvex mirror;

if living beings are treated as objects, will children prefer robots?

Evil's Impotence

Jehu, where is the house of Ahab,
Ba'asha—Jeroboam's line?
Evil contains within
the seeds of its own impotence.

The blood of Cain is
mingled on the spot where Abel fell,
Judas's thirty shekels dangle like treasonous
kisses above a potter's field.

Where, o where, in all Israel
is an obelisk for scarlet Jezebel?
Idols, though of no real substance,
do grievous injury to the soul.

While saints like Monarch butterflies
drink of Christ's red poison,
soon are swallowed up by predators,
who vomit up their godly serum.

Adam, taught to speak,

sought to curse both Pygmalion and Geppetto,

Lucifer, though once so bright,

radiates no inner prismatic splendor.

The king, seeing his reflection in a golden bowl,

like the slave before his wind-rippling mirror,

is Narcissus out of whack

and on the azure lip of extinction.

Postures

From my hammock
the world looks upside down,
the starry canopy above,
the moral magistrate within,
convince me of immortality.

Sitting in the lotus
I contemplate the two worlds
—artificial and real—
the first, concrete, plastic, ornate,
the second, mysterious, wild, untouched.

From my jungle gym hanging by my ankles,
I swing between fate and free will,
rational and determined,
I perceive a higher bar,
but my will falls short.

Riding a seesaw incline,
I tilt first toward intuition, then perception,
the knower and the object
part or merge,
in the end—I'm the voice of God.

In the spinning circle

I break off cults at every angle,

exhort my flock,

—and how many great thoughts

depend on a shift in weight?

Long-Awaited Rendezvous

Long-awaited rendezvous
almost invariably fail,
though pleasantries are touted,
surefire quips invoked,
there's a cascade of impromptu laughter,
extended flares of intimacy—
still, at the subatomic level,
one finds maneuvering, not attraction.

Why are romantics so bewitched
by a vision of colossi in dialogue,
since each is prone to one-upmanship, posturing,
under the strain of fragmented understanding
ebullient expectations die tumultuously,
so pen pals meet face-to-face, never again to correspond,
Augustine, eager to interrogate Manichean Faustus,
soon trotted off after a remote Galilean prophet.

How often the protégé is disappointed in his mentor,
the disciple by his guru,
no living being can possibly fulfill the hoopla
generated by a retinue of charismatic advance men,
recall how Van Gogh notched his ear at Gauguin's coming,

Melville was disenchanted by Hawthorne's aloofness,

Verlaine triggered Rimbaud,

ah! but our quest for bodhisattvas continues.

Blinding Revelation

We seek the dark when light is far too strong,
when blinding revelation suffuses every crack,
we grope for some unlit corner to continue our masquerade.

When yellow colors our somber salt-and-pepper,
we scuffle off toward curfews and commitments,
his countenance too harsh for Laodicean eyes.

    The rose wilts,
the cactus discards its green,
        the salamander, too, lurks behind the shadow of the rock,
and I would approach Mount Sinai
        with sandals all unloosened.

    Harbingers we permit,
portents and prophecies are allowed,
        avatars and gurus make few ripples,
but Everyman will not
        be upstaged by Sir Anthony Absolute.

    We are children of the gloom,
slumbering despite catastrophe,
    drunk halfway through dinner,
in a world of shining lanterns
    we unscrew bulbs and open circuits.

Half-Light

The blue before the dawn makes us wish for more,
so the hint of revelation Nature does disclose,
as with the wind-swept hem or the overflowing bodice,
sometimes half-light is worse than none.

Expectations raised can crash down with a thud,
better to be unevangelized than to apostatize,
half-light brings the guilt without the balm,
after the first touch, trees get up and walk.[7]

The prayers of those with faith, who will not persevere,
the impetus of those that dream success, yet never risk a thing,
the orator with his cache of illustrations, the songbird with his repertoire,
the pre-incarnate Word who has no unicorn.

Cosmetic preparation and the hesitating beau,
the sun cracking through the clouds: still no arc or band,
the first fish to walk upon the earth rumors, "What a farce,"
or, after landing on the moon, we scorn all other solar systems.

---

7. Mark 8:24.

A bill writ in water, an aperitif with no nightcap,
an execution pardon that a jailer has just now stashed,
pledges, self-exertion—grace that can't be bought—
forgive us our lukewarm passions, or Lord, spew us out.

Who Will Pass Judgment?

Quis custodiet ipsos custodes?
when they scribble out their scorecards,
tack up their statistical pegs,
when we cry out our egg carton holes,
like laboratory mice
lost in a stammering maze.

Who will pass verdict on the judges
when avarice and bias drip down their robes?
when they wink at dame justice
from behind their Roman private property rules?
when the hanged man on the tarot
is a milk-bane Ox-Bow?[8]

Who will critique the unknown Leonardos
when scholarly opinion defers?
when misunderstood genius
is bulldozed by the wastebasket load?
when all ballyhoo upright Germanicus
and slander psychotic Tiberius?

---

8. Clark, *Ox-Bow Incident*.

Who will cleave your hemisphere,
ratify your conscience or no,
pour in genes, education, and free will
and read out your magnetic morals?
determine your Hades, Tartarus, or Elysium
with omni-pure compassion and truth?

To Be a Woman

To be a woman in a woman's body
perhaps Tiresias has known,
to be hawked as a sideshow freak
by braggarts, sots, and pimps,
to be told to stay at home
and there be brutalized by violent men,
to feel shy, inferior, seductive,
to know not ambition's highest crown,
to veil seclusion with Arabic depression,
to sew and cook and wash
for the sons you bore and love,
to be prey to cyclical hurt and emotional bleeding,
fragile tears and glandular urges,
to be labeled "masculine," "bitch," if you resist,
"submissive sycophant," if you don't,
to silently suffer society's double standard
and end up a soft, smooth ellipsis
in an aggressive, dominant male herd.

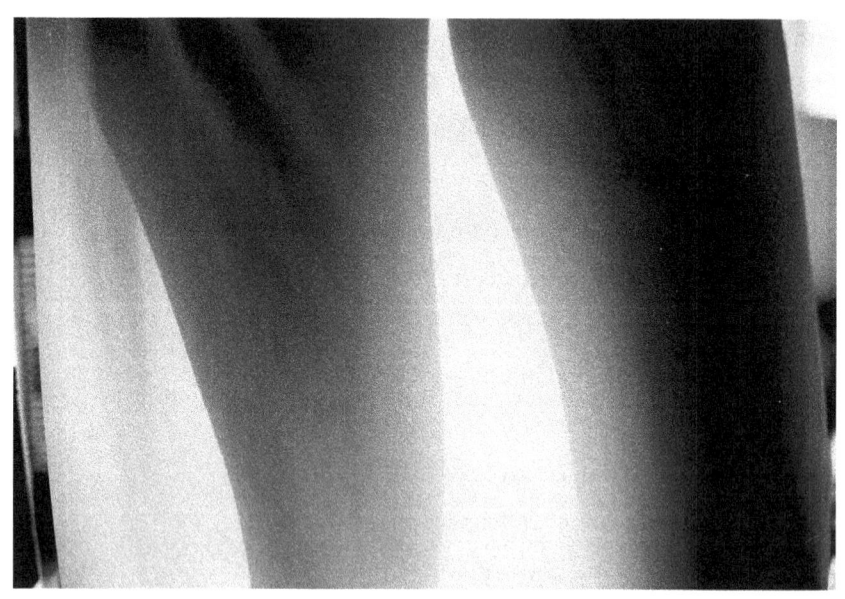

The Whimpering Victim

He pried me open like an oyster
to seize his precious pearl,
put on a rubber mask, breathed deep, then submerged,
surreptitious as a moray eel
gliding through murky trenches and canyons;
unprovoked, he struck—
pummeling my most sensitive fissures
with bone-wrenching fists and fingers,
pulling and pulling me apart as if with a winch
till I ached like a benumbed corpse.

I moaned,
then he unsheathed that fleshly dagger
and drove it home as if to still all uterine life,
relishing my dry, whimpering resistance,
afterwards he leered and spat,
tossed me aside like a porcelain doll,
while brandishing a hazardous blade
which he threatened to ram down some orifice
should I so much as Philomela peep,
then he strode outside with that smirk of an Olympic champion.

What grotesque rage

forced him to tear open my insides with his bare hands,

and what pornographic den

spawned these cruel, insatiable lusts,

which he practice-pretended on compliant whores,

yet was anxious to execute on the respectable—

those he scorned—

he loves overpowering the weak

and munching on pale, chaste meat,

how nauseatingly unreal.

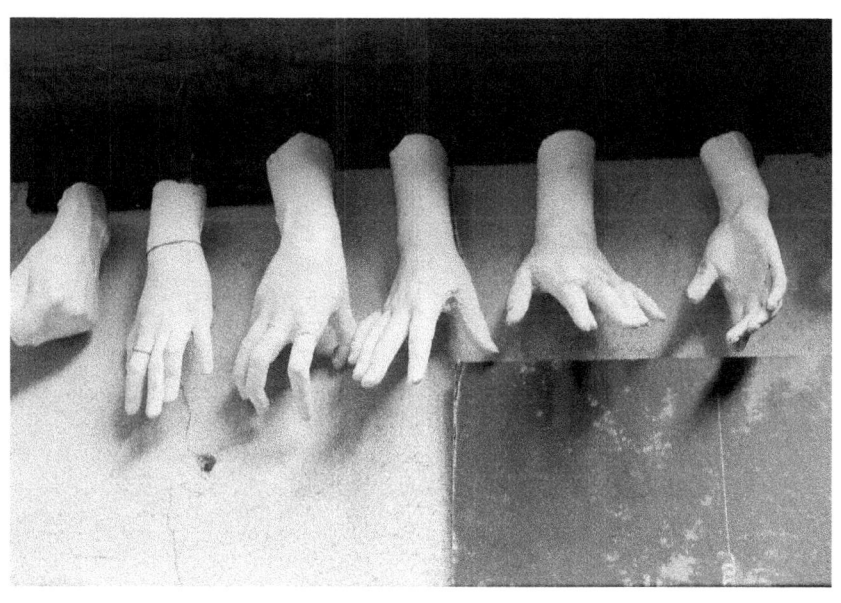

THE WRONGED

In an unguarded moment
I let my defenses down,
more vulnerable than a mollusk
outside its shell,
I was beaten and stabbed
till white corpuscles flowed.

For a few dollars and an upper
I was violated beyond repair,
like Solzhenitsyn, yes,
I remember the archipelago
(the rottenness of man)
and the inverted torch is my symbol.

Civilized?

Be a civilized man.

Join the Gestapo.

"Jew-das"

> "You should simply inquire:
> Is this or that man a threat to us? Then
> Is he a Jew?"—Bertolt Brecht[9]

or so my friends pronounce it,

long proboscis,

Christ-killing usurers,

open sore of medieval Christendom,

the locus of so many holocausts—

Alexandria, Toledo, Auschwitz—

olive skin, mustard badge,

herded into the gilded ghetto

to worship a monad God.

Maimonides, Spinoza,

Zohar, Kabbalah,

bouncy Hasidim, models for Rembrandt,

God's chosen, circumcised, covenant people,

the star of David jutting out against the minaret and spire,

fine country gents riding to a pogrom:

Pharaoh's Red Sea fiasco, if you smite God's holy ones,

prophetic antics: Zedekiah's iron horns, Jeremiah's wooden yoke.

---

9. Brecht, *Selected Poems*, 126–27, paraphrased.

So many times their seed has hung on Isaac's thread,

barred from intermarriage, government office,

and golf courses in Connecticut,

one roadblock to all ambition:

baptism and salvation,

yids and kikes and sacrificing babies,

the Protocols of the Elders of Zion,

—slander the alien and if he's uppity, torch 'im.

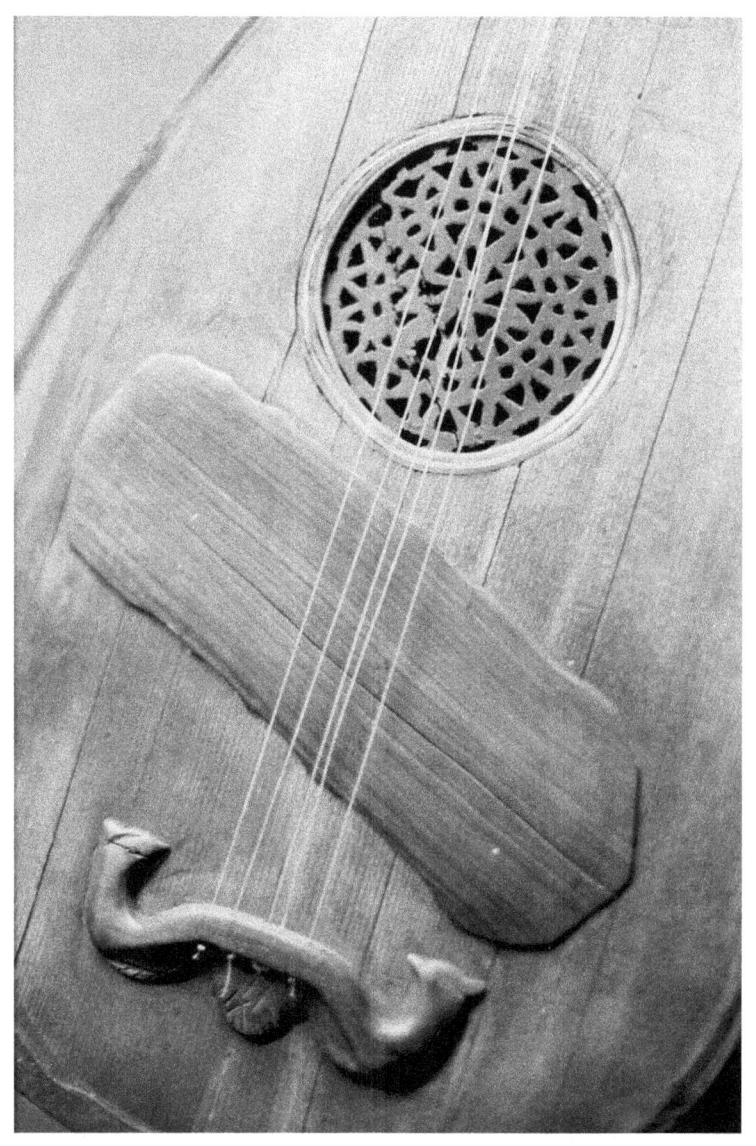

The Orchestra at Auschwitz

The orchestra at Auschwitz
led by whining Nero on his fiery fiddle
is conducting an all-Yiddish pogrom,
Kultur, Aufklärung, Gesellschaft
have succumbed to Hippocratic torture—
cyanide showers, nightshade ovens,
bones piled high as the Brandenburg gate.

The soothing strings, the wafting percussion
are drowned out by goose-stepping brass,
the French horns are one-upped by Viennese bassoons,
the Czech and Hungarian cellists
pizzicato-swoon alongside Hasidic violins,
a pink-triangled drummer goes haywire,
the flute trio resembles a tree of fallen angels.

The commandant requires his childhood favorite:
"Ride of the Valkyries" (through the Semitic killing fields),
nuances aren't so critical as Übermensch enthusiasm;
I can't bear the elongated scale of ironies,
the fortissimo sharp and flat fates,
no keyboard has that tragic a half-tone,
for these anguished dissonances are altogether inhumane.

East of Eden

there are volcanic fumes,
poisons, thistles, man-swallowing birds,
the garden mists anaconda cease
where a shadow's shadow falls.

Cain hired himself an architect,
tinsmiths, construction crews,
invented civilization to escape his guilt,
bore children with agonizing success,
depleted ecologies, exhausted this planet, "Earth,"

hunted species to extinction, strewed garbage
from Point Barrow to Cape Horn,
polluted the air with acid industrial rain,
ransacked Third World empires
to prettify his museum,

established a "fail-safe"
nuclear arsenal, invented nerve gas,
toxic formulas, like a common thug
held the world hostage or threatened
to blow it up to cosmic immortalize
his name—AMANITA VERNA.

East of Eden
ominous silence is punctuated by
indistinct echoes and high divorce,
battered children, husbands who renege,
police on the take, Sicilian loyalty oaths,

priests vying for the tiara,
deviance that would cause Freud to faint,
gaps in the tapes, guardian angels who fall
hard on the heels of each other,

artificial, blinking bulbs, man pillaging
man—war-like, estranged,
denying death with sleep-inducing
pills, scratchy gramophone disks,
south, southwest of peace.

Trinity Site, New Mexico

"Grant that Nagasaki may be the last atomic wilderness in the history of the world."—Takashi Nagai[10]

The sun is rising in the wrong direction
at Trinity Site, New Mexico,
exuberant physicists and bleary-eyed researchers
are experiencing fledgling technological guilt,
neutron particles endanger all human life,
Robert Oppenheimer and Edward Teller argue about mega-mega deaths.

The desert smells like bombarded plutonium,
white rain infects the spotted livestock,
Tierra del Fuego winds flatten the core,
scales of Hiroshima flesh
hang as if from an elephant man,
a meteoric fireball sears the mind.

Jittery Truman needs a quick fix—
believing history slants in the victor's favor—
generations will rise up and call Allied bombers blessed
and lose track of unpronounceable Japanese military objectives.

---

10. Nagai, *Bells of Nagasaki*, 118.

War will no longer wear a human aggressor's face,

just cold, calculated projection lights,

direct mushroom hits and civilian spillovers.

"I am become fallout, the radioactive destroyer of eons."

Death

Is death an open window
where souls escape from cloistered rooms,
or just another dead-end street
paved with pessimism?

who can say what mysteries might be unveiled
in God's expanding mind,
or whether only rotting carbon atoms
will stink up that abandoned lane?

won't someone scrape away my frosty pane,
or is it meant to be forever translucent,
reflecting back only what we want to see?

or can't someone drive past that foreboding sign,
reconnoiter the last few walled feet, dispel our hopes,
and stoically report back again?

why is it so hard for science to penetrate
this first and last frontier?

or hasn't Newton or Einstein
developed the ultimate equation
to explain life and death,
both here and hereafter?

The Soul & the Body

The soul has spatial limits,
the body is filled with an unrepeatable time.

Prisoners of Time

Time is an arrow
or is it an expanding circle
or a dot zig-zagging through apparent space?
does it have objective-subjective components?
of course, it can be charted by pendulum, shadow and dial,
or radiocarbon deterioration,
digital time itself is proportional,
regardless of the prelate's rage or the saint's desperation,
the earth spins precise as a chronometer.

Is time viscous
or carved into immovable stone,
are there gravity dips in the space-time continuum
or does it extend on for parsecs and parsecs
with no discernible Fraunhofer lines?
I know it's the dough we knead for our daily bread,
but is it Einstein absolute as the speed of light
or does time leak somewhere, somehow
into a black, indeterminate medium?

Could I replay one single instant,
pull back my headstrong king,
choose from a hypothetical series of outcomes with movable options
or is there just one set field to play on
and this down recorded for all eternity,
so all must deflect and triangulate accordingly?

There's an ongoing river of light in the night skies,
auguries of whirlpools and eddies,
dead spots in the maddening center of calm,
ultimate time is unattainable as that starlit shore,
yet the decisions we make today may be as momentous
as those determining infinite joy or unending pain.

The Cosmic Fall

Cracked bowl
of a planet,
fissure extraordinaire!
shifting plates
all out of whack,
bang! smash! pow!
oval wobbling in its orbit,
earth groggy from the blows.

an Incision of Evil
setting landmasses ablaze,
once a giant spinning top,
the embodiment of glee,
the Mirror of Three-dimensional Love,
now . . . smoldering rubble.

for twenty-five minutes
the brightest object in four galaxies:
Vegetation green
charred by Decadent black—
all that's left is the Cheshire smile.
Revolving carousel
mourns its half-second of naiveté.

Eve swallowed,
Adam stuttered,
the rest is history.

Demi-gods now rule
in a secular commonwealth:
the Garden,
a sprawling emptor-polis.

the Cosmic Breach:
why and wherefore?
    self-love,
    antinomianism,
    hubris,
    short-sightedness?

and how will it be repaired?
    animal sacrifice,
    penance,
    faith,
    flashes of mysticism?

the Drama of Redemption:
    Adam hid,
    God came looking;
    Adam lied,

God kept questioning;
        Adam persevered,
God starts punishing.

A round of denials
countered by unmerited reprieves.
Veni, redemptor gentium.

Free Will

Like streamers dangling on a string
waiting for the next gust to set them flapping,
like leaves carried forward by the momentum of eddies and tides
scraping against exposed ledges and jutting branches,
like pilgrims jostling toward some healing Lourdes
anxious to hurl tumors, crutches into a mausoleum,
like a Parisian mob seized by one collective passion,
whether to protest grievances or run riot and burn.

Are we adrift or the captains of our fate?
sociologists compile statistics,
logicians speak in entangled semantic webs,
are we part of some deterministic cube,
may an unseen hand be lifting us ever skyward,
is there one distinctive template inside the sperm?

I've pegged my life on the supposition
that the will is pliable, susceptible to change,
there's hope for the down-and-out
if they kick their deforming habits,
while those who are riding high
may yet taste the bitter fruit of their lack of restraint,
I believe one can never be counted out until his dying breath.

Gentleness and goodness plus a dose of exhortation—
there's an element of unpredictability in the rational heart—
the foregone conclusion, a mere cerebral construct,
can be toppled by a song,
it's never too late to accept the divine, "Yes,"
idle hands may yet set the world agawk.

History has never seen
all the whirlwinds one truly dedicated savant can create,
those who draw near are scorched by his flaming touch,
purified within his expanding parameters,
heat and light envelop entire continents, epochs;
resolute gambler, whoever you are, anxious for that one momentous strike,
you, too, may enter into Sinai's precincts,
fall stammering, lisping, incoherent under its searing beam.

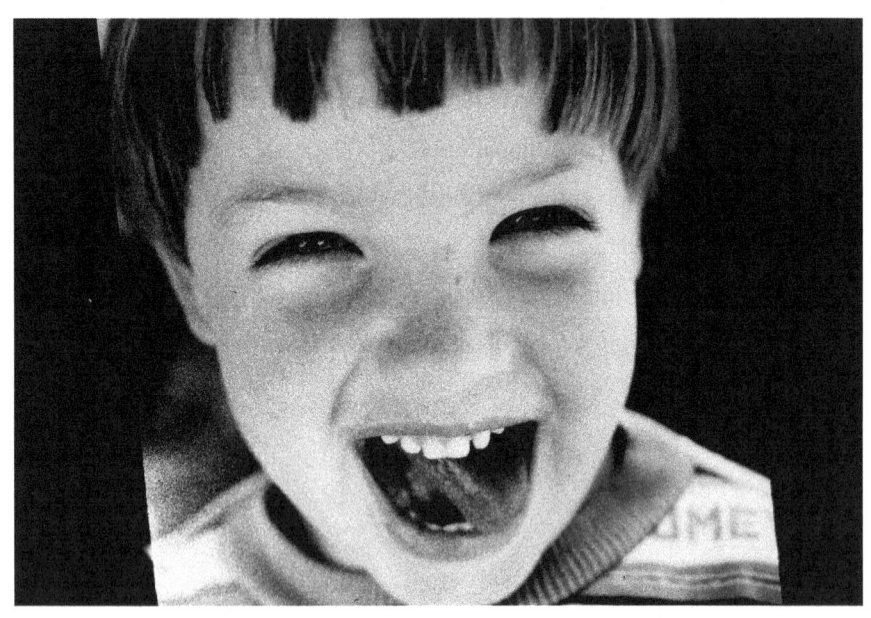

Questions

What is a heart that it moves our poets so?
What is life that it should flaunt Sheol?
What is a smile that bids all join its happy circle?
What is a tear but Nature's own safety valve?

What is man that he should be named earth's viceroy?
What is a woman that she should stand in as co-pilot?
What is a fetus that it so monopolizes our intentions?
What is a pupil but a storehouse of facts and theorems?

What is rhyme but a caveman's mnemonic tool?
What is a simile but the juxtaposition of incongruity?
What is a paradox but a polygon inscribed in a circle of truth?
What is synthesis? Why, Zeitgeist of conjecture, asserts Kuhn.[11]

What is God but the one pipe dream that's real?
What is Jesus but his own incarnate man?
What is the resurrection but the culminating act of his newest play?
What is heaven but the subconscious, unavowed goal of humanism?

---

11. Kuhn, *Structure of Scientific Revolutions*.

Solitude

Solitude

to dance with a butterfly.

Solitude

to restore specific gravity.

Solitude

to hear virtue crackling.

Solitude

to see my way to heaven.

Solitude

to recharge old power cells.

Solitude

to evade the congestion.

Solitude

to whistle our favorite melodies.

Solitude

to introspect my shadow.

Solitude

to protest worldly incursions.

Solitude

to transcend my *Sitz im Leben*.

Solitude

to concentrate on one's own creation.

Solitude

to ease Christ's agony.

Solitude

to refabricate the linings of the soul.

Solitude

to shake down old prejudices.

Solitude

to petition on behalf of our enemies.

Solitude

to be moral man in immoral society.

Solitude

to excavate virgin lanes.

Solitude

to chart abnormalities.

Solitude

to harmonize the basilisk and the porpoise.

Solitude

to steep oneself in God

All I Have

All I have is paper and ink,
a few stray thoughts which, if God wills,
may coalesce into a thing of profoundest beauty.

All I have is a Platonic form,
dedicated, experienced hands
anxious to shape a terra cotta facsimile.

All I have is a vibrating box,
a soul overflowing with psalms and heartfelt hymns
and a ready knack for making music.

All I need is a lithesome heart,
a mirroring empathy,
and an eagerness to help a hurting neighbor.

All I require—in terms of vocation—
is a dunghill and a pitchfork
to give him praise.

The Snow Falls Indifferently

The snow falls indifferently on the grand and the good,
prophets don't come with a mellifluous megaphone,
saints don't wear a countenance beaming with effervescence,
those who have accumulated merits aren't ravishing beauties,
the intelligent aren't branded with some benign sign of Cain,
the wise don't automatically assume postures of contemplation,
instead uprightness and evil spring from the selfsame clod,
invisible except to God's observant eye.

Nor do these manifestations awaken the world—
a tempest, an earthquake, a conflagration—
instead God appears as a still, small candle, barely an echo,
his presence is perceived as an absence,
as inconsequential as pouring wine during a wedding at Cana,
what could be more lowly than a Sovereign
who rules through unprepossessing intermediaries?

Certainly the earth would be a simpler, saner sphere,
if villains and heroes never fought heel-to-heel,
if Satan weren't an admirable, dashing flatterer,
if reward or punishment were issued following each tepid step,
but could character flourish in a cosmos of such insidious rules?
Ought we rather swear allegiance like those Magi of old

to some bursting nova,

move imperceptibly in the direction of its spreading glow

till its flickers and flares encompass all that is known?

Unapproachable Light

We shall grow old together,
you and I,
a new generation will discard
worn, tired hypotheses,
sneer at our palpable mistakes,
debunk the sheriffs, outlaws,
and courtroom justices we uplifted,
exhume our burial chambers
to filch what food and drink
our souls savored and required.

We shall softly fade into
realms of unapproachable light,
be metamorphosed and forget
those separation anxieties
encountered from our mother's breast,
beyond the caliper and luminous dial,
in that celestial Cluny
of decorated initials and iridescent mosaics,
we shall go mad with longing
for the fair Messiah.

Listing of Photographs

1. Tree with bite taken out of leaves [Always the Flaw]
2. Busts on table at Daniel Chester French studio [Homo Sapiens]
3. Two people on telephone, woman smoking [On Human Nature]
4. Passersby with reflections in mirrors [Life Is . . .]
5. Cat underneath broken-down car [The Longer I Live]
6. People in Chinatown through car window [The Selected Sayings of Confucius]
7. Lighted angels and Christmas tree at Rockefeller Center [Too Bright Are Our Infirm Desires]
8. Boy yawning among bystanders [All Things Wind Down]
9. Bird flying away from sailing ship [In the Words of Aurelius]
10. Older couple on boardwalk [Entropy]
11. Two pedestrians near striped wall [1985, or Life in the Suburbs]
12. Newport, Rhode Island, mansion in rain [Pleasantries]
13. View through window of farmer sitting down [For Chelsea]
14. Couple waiting for subway [On Persuading]
15. Man's face and body in mirrors [Paralysis]
16. Boy looking up from dark staircase [The Number of Man]
17. Vacancy sign alongside cracked window pane [Powder Keg Assertions]
18. Old cabin in the mountains [Why Call It a "Road"?]
19. Porthole windows on wall [Fortress Mentality]

Listing of Photographs

20. Fancy ceiling light with reflection [A Crystal Chandelier]
21. Reflection of Chinese woman who has mouth open [Babel]
22. Distorted face masks [*Semper Idem*]
23. Amish horse and buggy going through town [A Flatlander]
24. A silver and a white bust [The Mechanical Thinking Marvel]
25. Reflection of passersby in wavy water [Evil's Impotence]
26. Windsurfing on lake [Postures]
27. Man walking out of subway—shot from below [Long-Awaited Rendezvous]
28. Man looking at light reflecting off World Trade Towers [Blinding Revelation]
29. Woman seemingly imprisoned in reflection [Half-Light]
30. Tops of marble columns [Who Will Pass Judgment?]
31. Man and woman waiting at street corner [To Be a Woman]
32. Woman's legs in see-through dress [The Whimpering Victim]
33. Sculptured hands reaching down [THE WRONGED]
34. Orthodox Jew getting onto bus ["Jew-das"]
35. Close-up of stringed instrument [The Orchestra at Auschwitz]
36. Man walking below elevated train [East of Eden]
37. Karate and nuclear apocalypse posters [Trinity Site, New Mexico]
38. A hearse with open rear door [Death]
39. Gravestone of Father Nealy Brimmer with flowers [The Soul & the Body]
40. Pedestrians at 53rd and Lexington Avenue, New York City [Prisoners of Time]
41. Crack in the cement of a well house [The Cosmic Fall]
42. Reflection of photographer and street scene [Free Will]
43. Young boy smiling [Questions]
44. Silhouette of guy looking out of subway window [Solitude]
45. Man painting details on pottery [All I Have]

Listing of Photographs

46. Snow falling against a semi-trailer [The Snow Falls Indifferently]
47. Antique portraits of an elderly man and woman [Unapproachable Light]

Works Cited

Allen, Woody. *Three Films of Woody Allen: Zelig, Broadway Danny Rose, The Purple Rose of Cairo.* New York: Vintage, 1987.
Augustine. *Confessions: Books 9–13.* Translated by Carolyn J.B. Hammond. Cambridge: Harvard University Press, 2016.
Aurelius, Marcus. *Meditations.* Translated by Maxwell Staniforth. New York: Penguin, 2005.
———. *The Meditations.* Translated by G.M.A. Grube. Indianapolis: Bobbs-Merrill, 1975.
———. *The Meditations of Marcus Aurelius.* Translated by George Long. In The Stoic and Epicurean Philosophers, edited by Whitney J. Oates, 491–587. New York: Modern Library, 1957.
Babbage, Stuart Barton. *The Mark of Cain.* Grand Rapids: Eerdmans, 1966.
Blakemore, Colin. *Mechanics of the Mind.* New York: Cambridge University Press, 1978.
Bowring, John, ed. *The Works of Jeremy Bentham, Volume X: Memoirs.* New York: Russell & Russell, 1962.
Bradbury, Ray. *Martian Chronicles.* New York: Bantam, 1975.
Brecht, Bertolt. *Selected Poems.* Translated by H.R. Hays. New York: Grove, 1959.
Brown, Calvin S., ed. *The Reader's Companion to World Literature.* New York: New American Library, 1956.
Capote, Truman. *In Cold Blood: A True Account of a Multiple Murder and Its Consequences.* Harmondsworth, Middlesex: Penguin, 1971.
Cellini, Benvenuto. *Autobiography.* Translated by George Bull. New York: Penguin, 1980.
Chesterton, G.K. *The Autobiography of G.K. Chesterton.* San Francisco: Ignatius, 2006.
———. *The Penguin Complete Father Brown.* New York: Penguin, 1981.
———. *Saint Thomas Aquinas: "The Dumb Ox."* Garden City, NY: Image, 1956.
Chomsky, Noam. *Reflections on Language.* New York: Pantheon, 1975.
Clark, Walter Van Tilburg. *The Ox-Bow Incident.* New York: New American Library, 1960.
Clegg, Brian. *The God Effect: Quantum Entanglement, Science's Strangest Phenomenon.* New York: St. Martin's Griffin, 2009.
Coffin, Charles M., ed. *The Complete Poetry and Selected Prose of John Donne.* New York: Modern Library, 1952.
Collins, Francis S. *The Language of God: A Scientist Presents Evidence for Belief.* New York: Free Press, 2007.
Confucius. *The Analects.* Translated by D.C. Lau. London: Penguin, 1979.
———. *The Analects of Confucius.* Translated and annotated by Arthur Waley. New York: Vintage, 1938.

Works Cited

———. *Confucian Analects, The Great Learning and the Doctrine of the Mean*. Translated by James Legge. New York: Dover, 1971.

Cowan, Henry J., ed. *A Guide to the World's Greatest Buildings: Masterpieces of Architecture & Engineering*. San Francisco: Fog City, 2001.

Davids, Peter H. *The Epistle of James: A Commentary on the Greek Text*. Grand Rapids: Eerdmans, 1982.

Dodds, E.R. *Pagan and Christian in an Age of Anxiety*. New York: Norton, 1970.

Dostoyevsky, Fyodor. *The Brothers Karamazov, Volume 1*. Translated by David Magarshack. Baltimore: Penguin, 1970.

———. *Three Short Novels: Notes from Underground, Poor People, The Friend of the Family*. Translated by Constance Garnett. New York: Dell, 1973.

Dunning, A.J. *Extremes: Reflections on Human Behavior*. Translated by Johan Theron. New York: Harcourt Brace Jovanovich, 1992.

Eagleman, David. *The Brain: The Story of You*. New York: Vintage, 2017.

Editors of Christian History Magazine. *131 Christians Everyone Should Know*. Nashville: Broadman & Holman, 2000.

Ehrlich, Eugene. *Amo, Amas, Amat and More*. New York: Harper & Row, 1987.

Einstein, Albert. *Relativity: The Special and General Theory*. 16th ed. Translated by Robert W. Lawson. New York: Crown, 1961.

Ellsberg, Robert. *All Saints: Daily Reflections on Saints, Prophets, and Witnesses for Our Time*. New York: Crossroad, 1977.

Endicott, Norman J., ed. *The Prose of Sir Thomas Browne*. New York: Norton, 1972.

Frame, Donald M., trans. and ed. *Montaigne's Essays and Selected Writings: A Bi-lingual Edition*. New York: St. Martin's, 1963.

Freud, Sigmund. *Civilization and Its Discontents*. Translated by James Strachey. New York: Norton, 1961.

Gardner, Martin. *The Relativity Explosion, Completely Revised Edition*. New York: Vintage, 1976.

Goethe, Johann Wolfgang. "Egmont." Translated by Michael Hamburger. In *The Classic Theatre, Volume II: Five German Plays*, edited by Eric Bentley, 1–91. Garden City, NY: Doubleday, 1959.

———. *Selected Verse*. Translated and edited by David Luke. New York: Penguin, 1981.

Gould, Stephen Jay. *Ever Since Darwin: Reflections in Natural History*. New York: Norton, 1979.

Homer. *The Iliad*. Translated by W.H.D Rouse. New York: New American Library, 1938.

Jaspers, Karl. *Plato and Augustine*. Edited by Hannah Arendt. Translated by Ralph Mannheim. New York: Harcourt, Brace & World, 1962.

Kant, Immanuel. *Groundwork of the Metaphysics of Morals*. Translated by H.J. Paton. New York: Harper & Row, 1964.

———. *Religion Within the Limits of Reason Alone*. Translated by Theodore M. Green and Hoyt H. Hudson. New York: Harper & Row, 1960.

Kuhn, Thomas S. *The Structure of Scientific Revolutions*. Chicago: University of Chicago Press, 1962.

Lattimore, Richard, trans. *The Odes of Pindar*. Chicago: University of Chicago Press, 1959.

Nagai, Takashi. *The Bells of Nagasaki*. Translated by William Johnston. Tokyo: Kodansha, 1984.

Nicholas of Cusa. *Selected Spiritual Writings*. Translated by H. Lawrence Bond. Mahwah, NJ: Paulist, 1997.

Works Cited

Niebuhr, Reinhold. *Man's Nature and His Communities: Essays on the Dynamics and Enigmas of Man's Personal and Social Existence*. New York: Charles Scribner's Sons, 1965.

———. *Moral Man and Immoral Society: A Study in Ethics and Politics*. New York: Charles Scribner's Sons, 1960.

Pascal, Blaise. *Pensées*. Translated by A.J. Krailsheimer. Baltimore: Penguin, 1968.

———. *Pensées and Provincial Letters*. Translated by W.F. Trotter. New York: Modern Library, 1941.

Poe, Edgar Allen. *Complete Stories and Poems of Edgar Allen Poe*. Garden City, NY: Doubleday, 1966.

Pope, Alexander. *Selected Poetry and Prose*. Edited by William K. Wimsatt, Jr. New York: Holt, Rinehart, and Winston, 1964.

Rousseau, Jean-Jacques. *Emile*. Translated by Barbara Foxley. New York: Dutton, 1977.

Rutland, Robert A., ed. *The Papers of James Madison, Volume 10*. Chicago: University of Chicago Press, 1977.

Sacks, Oliver. *Hallucinations*. New York: Alfred A. Knopf, 2012.

Sartre, Jean-Paul. *Existentialism and Humanism*. Translated by Philip Mairet. Brooklyn: Haskell House, 1977.

Sophocles. *The Three Theban Plays*. Translated by Robert Fagles. New York: Penguin, 1984.

Steinbeck, John. *Novels 1942–1952*. Edited by Robert DeMott. New York: Viking, 2001.

Stevenson, Leslie and David L. Haberman. *Ten Theories of Human Nature*. 3rd ed. New York: Oxford University Press, 1998.

Tavris, Carol and Elliot Aronson. *Mistakes Were Made (But Not By Me)*. Rev. ed. Boston: Houghton Mifflin Harcourt, 2015.

Taylor, Jeremy. *The Rule and Exercises of Holy Living and The Rule and Exercises of Holy Dying*. London: Longmans, Green & Co., 1941.

Thoreau, Henry David. *Walden or, Life in the Woods*. New York: New American Library, 1960.

Tournier, Paul. *The Meaning of Persons*. Translated by Edwin Hudson. London: SCM Press, 1970.

———. *The Person Reborn*. Translated by Edwin Hudson. New York: Harper & Row, 1975.

Waley, Arthur, trans. *The Book of Songs*. New York: Grove, 1960.

United Nations Educational, Scientific and Cultural Organization. *World Heritage Sites: A Complete Guide to 936 UNESCO World Heritage Sites*. 4th ed. Buffalo: Firefly, 2011.

www.ingramcontent.com/pod-product-compliance
Lightning Source LLC
Chambersburg PA
CBHW071433160426
43195CB00013B/1880